FIDDLE DEE DEE RECIPES

A TASTE OF "GONE WITH THE WIND"

To my precious & loving son & daughter, Jimmy & Angie Sue
I hope you enjoy my labor of love!
Bunches of love!
Mom —

Leury Lynn Crane

BY TERRY LYNN CRANE

The author's use of references to the novel, *Gone With The Wind*, by Margaret Mitchell, and to its place names, characters and other elements are by permission of GWTW Partners, LLC.
Photo Credits – Licensed By: Warner Bros. Entertainment Inc. All Rights Reserved: p3, p11, p13, p14, p15, p19, p28, p38, p42(3), p46, p49, p55, p56, p63, p66(2). Licensed By: Fotolia inside cover, p20, p29. Licensed By: Lily Graison p30.
Miss Scarlett font trademarked and licensed by MyFonts for this purpose.
Front and back covers were illustrated by Terry Lynn Crane as well as all sketches of cast members of "Gone With The Wind" inside this book. All color graphics inside this book (except as noted) were designed by Alicia Reese Holloway. The book layout was designed by Terry Lynn Crane.

This book would not be possible without the help of the following people: Deacon Steve Swope, thank you for your direction and friendship. I know it was not a chance meeting in that little antique store in Danville, Kentucky. Paul Anderson, Jr., thank you for your gift of attention and assistance despite your extremely busy work schedule. Your assistance has been most appreciated. Julie Heath, thank you for your assistance and generosity. It was my sincere pleasure to work with you. Frank Crabtree, Sr., thank you for your love, support and for reminding me how important patience is. I love you very much. Barbara Halfacre, thank you for always encouraging me to reach for my dreams. You have always been there through all the mountains and valleys. I love you with all my heart, Mama. Alicia Holloway, you're like a sister to me. Thank you for all your help and the many hours you spent designing the graphics for this book. You are truly an angel on earth. I love you. Vivienne St. Clair, thank you for assisting with the lettering on the cover and spine. I appreciate you so much! Patti Ann Bengen, thank you for your friendship, honorary sisterhood and hours of conversation. You are an enormous inspiration to me. Thank you for your guidance and for believing in this project. I love you. Matt Conlon, thank you for your friendship, assistance and guidance. I appreciate you so much. Amy Nutzell, my precious friend and sister girl, thank you for being my personal "dream weaver".

Copyright © 2014 Terry Lynn Crane All Rights Reserved.
Published in the USA by: Gibson-Ragle Publishing Co., P.O. Box 21, Bronston, Kentucky 42518
No part of this book may be reproduced (except for inclusion in reviews), disseminated or utilized in any form or by any means, electronic or mechanical, including, photocopying, recording, or in any information storage and retrieval system, or the Internet/World Wide Web without written permission from the author or publisher.
For further information, please contact: luvgwtw2@yahoo.com
Fiddle Dee Dee Recipes A Taste of "Gone With The Wind"
Terry Lynn Crane
1. Title   2. Author   3. Cooking and Performing Arts
Library of Congress Control Number: 0019010124
ISBN 978-0-692-40475-1   Website: www.terrylynncrane.com   Printed in China

Dedicated to the memory of my late husband, loyal friend and loving companion, Fred Crane, "Fede".

Our adventures were many and the memories of our time together will forever be etched into my heart—as you are.

With love and admiration,
Terry Lynn
   Your "Terresita Muñequita"

TABLE OF CONTENTS

APPETIZERS & HORS D'OEUVRES

Jeems' Ham Roll-Ups	11
Jonas Wilkerson's Devilish Eggs	12
Melanie's Cheese Ball	13
Scarlett's Sausage Cheese Balls	14
Stuart Tarleton's Tapenade	15
Uncle Peter's Chicken Salad Balls	16

BEVERAGES

Aunt Pittypat's Holiday Cider	18
Brent's Mint Julep	19
Pretty In Pink Punch	20

TABLE OF CONTENTS

BREADS
Belle's Best Buttery Biscuits	23
Mammy's Short'nin' Bread	24
Southern Corn Pone	25

BREAKFAST
Bonnie's Egg Blossoms	27
Civil War Johnny Cakes	28
Fanny Elsing's Fried Apples	29
Frank's Frittata	30
Scarlett's Sausage and Apples	31
Tarleton Oaks' Breakfast Casserole	32
Tarleton Oaks' Breakfast Pizza	33

DESSERTS & SWEETS
Aunt Pittypat's Applesauce Cookies	35
Belle's Buttermilk Pie	36
Bonnie's Best Ever Chocolate Cake	37
Charles' Favorite Coconut Pie	38
Gerald's Ginger Bread	39
Prissy's Peanut Butter Pie	40
Scarlett's Skillet Chocolate Pie	41

HIGH TEA DELICACIES
Carreen's Chicken Curry Tea Sandwiches	46
Ellen's Artichoke Tea Sandwiches	47
Emmy's Egg & Olive Tea Sandwiches	48
Suellen's Smoked Salmon Sandwiches	49

MEATS & MAIN ENTREES
Ashley's Barbecued Chicken	51
Melanie's Marinated Steak	52
Pork's Plantation Pork Chops	53
Rhett's New Orleans Pot Roast	54
Twelve Oaks' Short Rib Barbecue	55

SALADS & SOUPS
Dolly's Eight Layer Salad	58
India's Cream Of Broccoli Soup	59
Plantation Potato Salad	60

VEGETABLES
Brent's Baked Beans	63
Carreen's Glazed Carrots	64
Dr. Meade's Dandy Dutch Lettuce	65

Authoress, Margaret Mitchell, never realized what an enduring legacy she would leave the world when she penned the novel, GONE WITH THE WIND, which was first published in May of 1936. It contains qualities of romanticism and archetypical characters with which most of us can relate. Thus, these universal qualities contribute to the lasting fascination of GONE WITH THE WIND with people of all ages, from all walks of life and in every country of the world.

FIDDLE DEE DEE RECIPES—A TASTE OF "GONE WITH THE WIND" celebrates this magnificent novel and movie. In this unique cookbook, a variety of recipes are offered from 1861-1873 in which GONE WITH THE WIND was set, as well as our own recipes which were served to family, friends and guests at our establishment, Tarleton Oaks Bed and Breakfast.

With a vision of opening a Gone With The Wind-themed bed and breakfast in Georgia, my late husband, Fred Crane, and I found a beautiful, antebellum home, circa 1849, listed on The National Register of Historic Places that had served as a Confederate headquarters and hospital during The War Between The States. We purchased the historic home on February 14, 2000---a beautiful Valentine's present to each other.

On June 30, 2000, after restoring this grand, Georgian Revival home, we opened Tarleton Oaks Bed and Breakfast, named appropriately for Fred's role, "Brent Tarleton", one of "Scarlett O'Hara's" suitors in David O. Selznick's classic 1939 movie, "Gone With The Wind". Throughout Tarleton Oaks' wide, central hallways, our memorabilia collection was displayed which contained over 100 personal items and costumes owned and worn by Vivien Leigh, Clark Gable, Olivia de Havilland, Leslie Howard, Butterfly McQueen, George Reeves and David O. Selznick, as well as autographed photos of most of the cast and crew of "Gone With The Wind". Our collection came to be known as The Gone With The Wind Hall of Stars Museum. We had the immense pleasure and privilege of meeting and visiting with amazing guests from all over the world during our tenure as innkeepers---an experience fondly remembered.

Mildred "Mammy" Murphy bore a striking resemblance to Hattie McDaniel, the actress who portrayed "Mammy" in "Gone With The Wind", and charmed our guests with her darling, outgoing personality. She wore a long, black dress with a white collar and apron. With a wide, friendly grin on her face, Mildred opened the front door and greeted our guests with "Welcome to Tarleton Oaks!" Then she warmly invited them inside. As she walked, she rustled her red, taffeta petticoat. She never failed to expose a little bit of the ruffled petticoat to our guests. Then, she'd call out, "Mr. Brent, Miz Terry, your guests iz here!" Mildred absolutely loved our guests, and our guests loved her! She always looked forward to portraying "Mammy" and truly enjoyed entertaining and talking to everyone. Sometimes, she would delight our guests by treating them to a solo performance of a spiritual song she had sung in church.

A stay at Tarleton Oaks included a comfortable room decorated in period antiques with a sitting area and private bath. In the guest rooms, which were named after GONE WITH THE WIND characters, a plate of delectable goodies awaited them. In the afternoon, I conducted a 2-hour tour of the home and museum. Then, later that evening, Fred personally narrated a 3-hour slide presentation of rare photography from "Gone With The Wind" and entertained questions from our guests. A gourmet breakfast was served on china in the Tara Dining Room at 9:00am the following morning. We so delighted in the togetherness with each guest in our home. Our slogan was "Tarleton Oaks Bed and Breakfast---a gateway to a bygone era where southern hospitality is NOT gone with the wind." Our earnest desire was to offer each guest a unique "Gone With The Wind" experience while we enjoyed spoiling them rotten. We felt so honored and blessed to have had this wonderful opportunity. The multiple return visits from many of our guests allowed us to make some truly, wonderful friends.

It is with sincere pleasure that I share these recipes with you, as well as special selections from our Gone With The Wind Hall of Stars memorabilia collection, which are intertwined with some treasured memories of our extraordinary experiences at Tarleton Oaks Bed and Breakfast. Bon appétit, y'all!

JEEMS' HAM ROLL-UPS

1 (8 ounce) package of cream cheese
1/8 teaspoon seasoning salt
1 medium jar whole dill pickles
2 packages of ham luncheon meat

Mix seasoning salt with the cream cheese. Spread a thin layer of this cream cheese mixture on a slice of ham and place a dill pickle on top. Roll up and place in the refrigerator for several hours. Slice in ½ inch pieces and serve promptly.

This is an extremely, rare photograph of Fred Crane, Ben Carter and George Reeves. Ben portrayed "Jeems", the Tarleton Twins' groomsman in "Gone With The Wind". Due to the enormous length of the film, this scene was cut. Ben Carter does not appear in the movie at all. He often portrayed an obliging domestic in Hollywood films, but, later, became one of the few black agents dedicated to promoting the careers of some of Hollywood's most celebrated actors and actresses of color, such as Hattie McDaniel, Eddie "Rochester" Anderson, Lena Horne and the Dandridge Sisters.

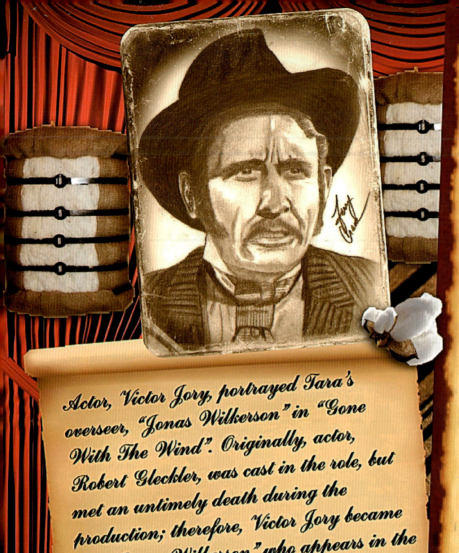

Actor, Victor Jory, portrayed Tara's overseer, "Jonas Wilkerson" in "Gone With The Wind". Originally, actor, Robert Gleckler, was cast in the role, but met an untimely death during the production; therefore, Victor Jory became the "Jonas Wilkerson" who appears in the movie. All scenes containing Gleckler had to be reshot. Victor was an excellent character actor and played the "heavy" or villain in many films.

JONAS WILKERSON'S DEVILISH EGGS

1 dozen large eggs
1 teaspoon baking soda
½ cup mayonnaise
1 tablespoon prepared mustard
6 pieces bacon (crispy)
shredded cheddar cheese (optional)

Place eggs in medium pot and cover with cold water. Add 1 teaspoon of baking soda. (The baking soda added to the water helps to make peeling the eggs much easier.) Bring water to a boil. Remove from heat and leave eggs covered for 20 minutes. (The eggs will continue to cook in the hot water.) Remove boiled eggs from the pot and immerse in cold water for a few minutes before peeling. Peel eggs and cut in half lengthwise. Place yolks into a mixing bowl. Smash and stir the yolks until smooth. Add mayonnaise, mustard and 6 tablespoons cooked chopped bacon and mix until smooth. Fill the empty egg whites with the egg mixture by teaspoonfuls. A trick is to get a small plastic storage bag and clip a tiny hole in one of the corners. Spoon the yolk mixture into the bag. Holding the bag, squeeze desired amount into empty egg whites. Garnish with crispy bacon pieces and sprinkle with shredded cheddar cheese.

Having read the novel, lovely Olivia de Havilland knew she could bring the character of "Melanie Hamilton Wilkes" to life on the big screen. Her sister, actress, Joan Fontaine, was approached by director, George Cukor, to audition for the role. Interested more in portraying "Scarlett", Fontaine turned him down and said, "Why don't you offer the role to my sister, Olivia. She wants the part." Olivia was under contract to Warner Brothers. Jack Warner did not want to loan her to Selznick; so, Olivia secretly met with Jack Warner's wife, Ann, and she convinced her husband to loan her after all. James Stewart was loaned to Warner Brothers in return.

MELANIE'S CHEESE BALL

2 (8 ounce) packages cream cheese
2 cups sharp cheddar cheese (grated)
1 tablespoon pimento (chopped)
1 tablespoon bell pepper (chopped)
1 tablespoon onion (finely chopped)
1 tablespoon Worcestershire Sauce
1 teaspoon lemon juice
dash of red pepper
½ cup pecans (finely chopped)

Combine cream cheese and sharp cheddar cheese. Then mix until well-blended. Add remaining ingredients (except pecans) and mix well. Shape into a ball and then roll the ball into pecans. Chill and serve with crackers. Wonderful served with grapes on the side.

SCARLETT'S SAUSAGE CHEESE BALLS

1 pound pork sausage
4 cups sharp cheddar cheese (grated)
½ cup celery (finely chopped)
1 ½ cup self-rising flour
½ cup onion (finely chopped)
½ teaspoon garlic powder

Preheat oven to 350 degrees F. Mix sausage and cheese. Blend well. Add flour and other ingredients, mix thoroughly. Bake on an ungreased cookie sheet for 15 minutes or until golden brown. Yields 6 dozen.

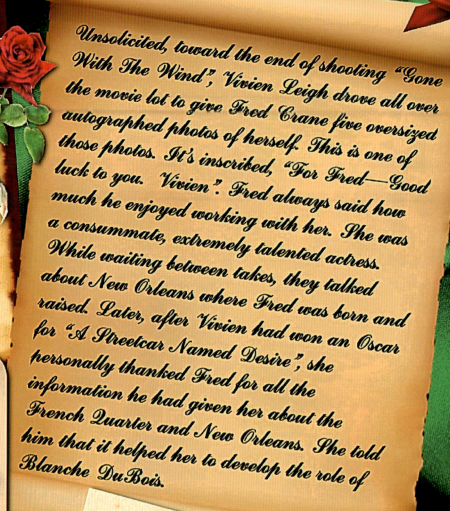

Unsolicited, toward the end of shooting "Gone With The Wind", Vivien Leigh drove all over the movie lot to give Fred Crane five oversized autographed photos of herself. This is one of those photos. It's inscribed, "For Fred—Good luck to you. Vivien". Fred always said how much he enjoyed working with her. She was a consummate, extremely talented actress. While waiting between takes, they talked about New Orleans where Fred was born and raised. Later, after Vivien had won an Oscar for "A Streetcar Named Desire", she personally thanked Fred for all the information he had given her about the French Quarter and New Orleans. She told him that it helped her to develop the role of Blanche DuBois.

STUART TARLETON'S TAPENADE

1 can (2.25 ounces) of black olives
1 bottle (5.75 ounces) of green olives with pimentos
2 tablespoons chopped garlic
1 tablespoon parsley flakes
2 tablespoons capers in Sherry Vinegar
3 tablespoons extra virgin olive oil
½ sweet onion

Finely chop black olives, green olives, pimentos, garlic, capers and sweet onion. Add parsley flakes and extra-virgin olive oil. Mix all ingredients, store in bottle or air tight container and refrigerate. This is a wonderful topping on full-bodied bread such as toasted Ciabatta Bread and makes a delicious hors d'oeuvre.

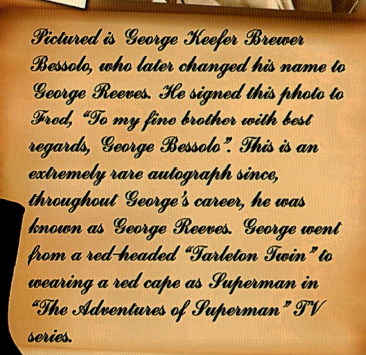

Pictured is George Keefer Brewer Bessolo, who later changed his name to George Reeves. He signed this photo to Fred, "To my fine brother with best regards, George Bessolo". This is an extremely rare autograph since, throughout George's career, he was known as George Reeves. George went from a red-headed "Tarleton Twin" to wearing a red cape as Superman in "The Adventures of Superman" TV series.

Eddie "Rochester" Anderson portrayed "Aunt Pittypat Hamilton's" Coachman, "Uncle Peter". His trademark "raspy" voice was due to hawking newspapers at the age of 12 which damaged his vocal cords. One of my favorite "Uncle Peter" scenes was when he was chasing the skinny, uppity rooster to have for Christmas dinner. Eddie Anderson had a long run on "The Jack Benny Show" as the beloved character, "Rochester", Benny's Valet. Fred was performing a Lucky Strike commercial for "The Jack Benny Show" and ran into Eddie on the set. Fred said, "Eddie, you're the berries!" (a term taken from a popular song at the time). Eddie never missed a beat and replied, "Yeah, the rasp-berries!"

UNCLE PETER'S CHICKEN SALAD BALLS

2 chicken breasts (boiled and finely chopped)
¼ teaspoon red pepper
1 tablespoon onion (finely chopped)
1 tablespoon pimento (chopped)
½ cup mayonnaise
1 cup pecans (chopped)

Mix all ingredients (except for pecans) and roll into small balls. Then, roll balls in chopped pecans. Chill and serve with rye bread.

Laura Hope Crews portrayed "Aunt Pittypat Hamilton", the flighty, spinster aunt who could faint at the drop of a hat. She was a long-time veteran of the theatre and films at the time "Gone With The Wind" was filmed. She began her career as a voice coach, but considered herself a stage actress. She was instrumental in discovering actress, Bette Davis, while Davis was working as an usher at the Cape Playhouse in Dennis, Massachusetts. Crews needed an additional actress for a play she was directing there and Bette Davis was asked to audition for the part. The rest is history.

AUNT PITTYPAT'S HOLIDAY CIDER

2 quarts apple cider
1 lemon sliced
juice of 3 lemons
1 cup sugar
cinnamon sticks

Combine apple cider, lemon juice, sugar and mix well. Heat the mixture and place lemon slices on top. Serve hot with a stick of cinnamon.

In the opening scene, one sees the back of Fred Crane "Brent Tarleton", and, as he turns, he is seen holding a Mint Julep in one hand as he's delivering the opening lines in "Gone With The Wind". A piece of trivia—in the picture, the credits are incorrect. They should read: "Brent Tarleton—Fred Crane", but, instead, they read, "Brent Tarleton—George Reeves". Also, Fred should be listed at the top of the credits since he spoke the opening lines. In the dialogue between "Scarlett" and the "Tarleton Twins", George Reeves "Stuart" refers to Fred as "Brent". So how could George be "Brent"? Fred and George looked so similar that even the cast and crew had a difficult time telling them apart.

BRENT'S MINT JULEP

4 fresh mint sprigs
2 ½ ounces bourbon whiskey
1 teaspoon powdered sugar
2 teaspoons water

Mix the mint leaves, powdered sugar and water in a 12 ounce glass or Collins glass. Fill the glass with shaved or crushed ice and add bourbon. Top with additional ice and finish by garnishing with a mint sprig. Serve with a straw.

Pretty Marcella Martin is one of only a few southern girls brought to Hollywood to be screen-tested as a candidate for the role of "Scarlett". Marcella tested twice for the part. She also assisted other actresses by reading the parts of "Scarlett" and "Melanie" in some screen tests for other people. While she did not win the role of "Scarlett", she was given the supporting role of "Cathleen Calvert". You will remember her as the young lady walking up the staircase at Twelve Oaks with "Scarlett" and informing her about "Rhett Butler's" terrible reputation. Marcella is credited with two other films, "The Man Who Returned To Life", "West of Tombstone" and one television episode of "The FBI".

PRETTY IN PINK PUNCH

1 can pineapple juice (46 ounces)
1 cup sugar
1 quart cranberry juice
2 quarts ginger ale
1 lemon
1 jar maraschino cherries
purified water

Create an ice ring by slicing up one lemon and pouring a jar of maraschino cherries into a round mold. Add enough purified water into the mold to almost fill it up and freeze. When you are ready to serve the punch, release the ice ring into a punch bowl and mix the pineapple juice, sugar, cranberry juice and ginger ale together. Pour carefully over the ice ring.

Marcella Martin

BREADS

BELLE'S BEST BUTTERY BISCUITS

¼ cup butter (melted)
2 cups baking mix
½ cup sour cream
½ cup lemon/lime-type soda (room temperature)
1 pinch of salt
½ cup self-rising flour (to use when patting out dough)

Preheat oven to 425 degrees F. Cut the sour cream into baking mix using a wooden spoon. (Do not use mixer.) Stir in ½ cup lemon/lime soda. The dough will be very soft and gooey. Sprinkle self-rising flour onto your bread board covered with wax paper. Knead and fold dough gently until coated with flour. (Do not over knead or this will make the biscuits tough. No rolling pin is needed.) Cut biscuits out with a biscuit cutter. Put butter in a 9-inch square clear glass casserole dish or cast iron skillet and place in the oven until melted. (Keep a close eye on it so that you are careful not to burn the butter.) Place cut biscuits in casserole dish on top of melted butter and turn over once to coat the biscuits on both sides. Place on middle oven rack. Bake for about 12-13 minutes or until lightly brown. These are some of the best biscuits you will ever eat! Yum!

Before Ona Munson was cast as "Belle Watling", some of the better known contenders for the role were Mae West, Tallulah Bankhead, (who refused the role because she felt the part was too small), Joan Blondell, Ann Sheridan, Loretta Young and Minna Gombel. Minna Gombel wanted the part so much that she wrote to Chaw Mank, a Hollywood Gossip Writer, "Chaw, why don't you tell all my fans to write to the Selznick Studios and tell them that they want to see me play the part of "Belle Watling" in "Gone With The Wind". It backfired on her when he actually printed her letter to him verbatim.

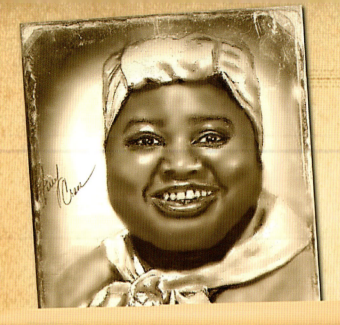

MAMMY'S SHORT'NIN' BREAD

2 cups all-purpose flour
1 ½ teaspoons baking soda
½ teaspoon ground cinnamon
¼ teaspoon ground nutmeg
½ cup buttermilk
¼ cup plus 2 tablespoons butter
1 cup molasses
1 egg (slightly beaten)

Preheat oven to 350 degrees F. Combine flour, cinnamon and nutmeg in a large mixing bowl. Blend well and set aside. Dissolve baking soda in buttermilk and set aside. Combine butter and molasses in a heavy saucepan and bring to a boil, stirring constantly. Add the flour mixture. Stir in buttermilk and egg. Pour batter into a greased and floured 10-inch iron skillet. Bake for 25 to 30 minutes or until toothpick inserted in the center comes out clean. Cool in skillet for 10 minutes. Take knife and slide around the outer edge and invert onto a plate. Slice in pie-shaped wedges.

Beloved Hattie McDaniel was a talented singer as well as an accomplished actress. She was the first woman of color to win an Academy Award. She won Best Supporting Actress in 1940 for her brilliant portrayal of "Mammy" in "Gone With The Wind". She had appeared as a domestic in about 40 films before she landed the role of "Mammy". She had the wonderful steadfast tenacity to diminish the egregious prejudice of color. She became the object of intense criticism by progressive blacks. She replied, "I'd rather make $700 a week playing a maid than $7 being one!"

SOUTHERN CORN PONE

¼ cup vegetable shortening
1 ½ cups white cornmeal
1 ½ teaspoons salt
1 1/3 cups buttermilk
2 eggs
½ cup melted butter (optional)

Preheat oven to 425 degrees F. Place a 9-inch cast iron skillet with ¼ cup vegetable shortening on the center rack. While the shortening is heating, mix together cornmeal and salt in a medium bowl. Add eggs and buttermilk, then mix together to make a thin batter. Carefully remove the cast iron skillet with hot, melted shortening (which has been in the oven for about ten minutes). Carefully pour the batter into the hot skillet. Bake the corn pone until a toothpick inserted in the center comes out clean (approximately 20 to 25 minutes). To brown, turn the oven to broil in order to brown the top. Keep a close eye on it to make sure it doesn't burn. Remove the skillet from the oven, slide a knife around the outer edges of the skillet and carefully shake the pan to loosen the corn pone from the skillet. Turn out onto a plate. If desire, drizzle melted butter on the top and serve hot. This is delicious with sorghum or honey.

BONNIE'S EGG BLOSSOMS

4 sheets phyllo dough pastry
2 teaspoons butter (melted)
4 teaspoons parmesan cheese (grated)
4 large eggs
4 teaspoons green onions (minced)
salt and black pepper to taste
parsley
Knorr Béarnaise Sauce (1 package)

Prepare Béarnaise Sauce as per directions on Knorr package and set aside. Preheat oven to 350 degrees F. Grease four (2½ inch) muffin cups. Brush 1 sheet of phyllo dough with butter. Top with another sheet, brush with butter. Cut the stack into six (4 inch) squares. Repeat with remaining 2 sheets. Stack three squares together, rotating so that the corners do not overlap. Press into prepared muffin or cup. Repeat with remaining squares. Sprinkle 1 teaspoon parmesan cheese into each phyllo dough-lined cup. Break 1 egg into each cup. Sprinkle minced green onion over egg. Season with salt and pepper. Bake 15 to 20 minutes or until the pastry is golden and eggs are set. Serve with Béarnaise Sauce spooned over the top. Garnish with fresh parsley. These are adorable and were very popular with our guests at Tarleton Oaks.

Darling Eleanor Cammack King portrayed "Eugenia Victoria Bonnie Blue Butler", the daughter of "Scarlett" and "Rhett" in "Gone With The Wind". Her step-father was Herbert Kalmus, a scientist, who co-founded Technicolor, a color motion picture process invented in 1916. In 1942, Cammie was cast as the voice of "Faline", the female fawn, in Walt Disney's animated movie, "Bambi". Cammie was extremely popular with the fans. She was always so gracious to talk to them and sign autographs. Dolls were also made in her likeness by Madame Alexander and World Dolls. In 2009, Cammie penned her memoir, Bonnie Blue Butler: A Gone With The Wind Memoir, before her passing in 2010.

Love to Terry & Fred
Cammie King

Frank "Junior" Coghlan had a long career as an actor. He starred in 129 films and was one of the child actors in the early "Our Gang" series. Junior was not credited in "Gone With The Wind", even though he portrayed the collapsing southern soldier. Coghlan had a line, "Put me down, put me down, damn ya! I can walk!" as he was being carried off the battlefield. Ironically, this preceded Clark Gable's line in which he says "damn". However, Junior's line was cut from the film. Later, one of his well-known roles was as "Captain Marvel". This led to a cult following and catapulted Coghlan into stardom. He was quoted, "There's a whole cult of people out there who are fascinated by "Captain Marvel". I'm getting invited to a lot more things these days. They think I'm a celebrity!"

CIVIL WAR JOHNNY CAKES

1 cup water
½ cups ground yellow cornmeal
½ teaspoon salt
½ cup milk
2 tablespoons butter
syrup, molasses or preserves for topping

Bring one cup of water to a boil in a medium saucepan. Combine the cornmeal, salt, boiled water and milk in a medium bowl. Stir well. Melt 2 tablespoons butter in a skillet or griddle over medium heat. Pour 1 tablespoon of batter into the skillet (pancake-style) to cook. Let it cook for 4 to 5 minutes on each side until its edges are lacy and lightly browned using a spatula to turn. Serve hot with butter, molasses, maple syrup or preserves.

FANNY ELSING'S FRIED APPLES

5 tart cooking apples 1 cup brown sugar
4+ tablespoons butter ½ teaspoon nutmeg

Wash, core and slice apples into 12-16 narrow wedges. Do not peel. Melt butter in a skillet or cast iron pan and add the apples. Cover the skillet and cook them for 5 minutes over medium-low heat. Continuously stirring, add in brown sugar and nutmeg. Stir well. Continue cooking the apples (covered) for 10 to 12 minutes or until the apples are tender. Check every few minutes while cooking. Add additional butter or water, if needed, to prevent the apples from sticking.

Carroll Nye
"Frank Kennedy"

FRANK'S FRITTATA

5 eggs
¼ cup milk
2 tablespoons parmesan cheese (grated)
½ teaspoon dried oregano leaves
½ teaspoon black pepper
1 pound pork sausage (mild) or to your taste
2 tablespoons butter
1 zucchini (1 cup sliced)
½ cup sliced green onions with green tops
¾ cup swiss cheese (shredded)

In a medium bowl, whisk eggs. Stir in milk, parmesan cheese, oregano and peppers. Set aside. Cook sausage in large skillet over medium heat until browned. Break up into small pieces as you cook. Drain. Remove sausage. Melt butter in same skillet. Add zucchini, shredded carrots and onions. Stir and sauté over medium heat until tender. Top with sausage, then swiss cheese. Pour egg mixture on top. Stir gently to combine. Cook, without stirring, over low heat for 8 to 10 minutes or until center is almost set. Remove from heat. Let stand for 5 minutes before cutting into wedges (like a pizza). Serve hot. Refrigerate leftovers. Recipe yields 4 to 6 servings.

Carroll Nye, who portrayed "Scarlett O'Hara's" second husband, "Frank Kennedy", appeared in 28 films between 1925 and 1944. He was also a radio editor for the <u>Los Angeles Times</u>, a broadcaster and an executive in public relations for The American Broadcasting Company. His brother, Ben Nye, was a make-up artist under Monty Westmore during the filming of "Gone With The Wind" and also for 20th Century Fox.

Vivien Leigh was born Vivian Mary Hartley in Darjeeling, India to British parents. She portrayed the lovely, flirtatious, head-strong, southern belle, "Scarlett O'Hara" in "Gone With The Wind". The role of "Scarlett" was the most sought-after by many of Hollywood's actresses. David Selznick began production on "GWTW" before the role of "Scarlett" was actually cast. During the burning of the Atlanta depot scene, Selznick's brother, Myron, brought Vivien Leigh and Laurence Olivier (who were in a relationship at the time) to the filming that evening. The yellow flames, that engulfed the buildings on the set, reflected in Vivien's blue eyes and made them appear green. Myron yelled to his brother, "Hey, Genius! Meet your 'Scarlett O'Hara'!" David was captivated and thought, "Now, if only she can act!"

SCARLETT'S SAUSAGE & APPLES

1 pound pork sausage
3 apples
½ stick butter
½ cup light brown sugar
1 tablespoon cinnamon

Form sausage into patties and fry lightly in a pan until just browned. Remove the sausage and drain the fat. Melt some butter in a pan (enough to barely cover the bottom). Core and slice three apples to a thickness of about ¼ inch, place in pan and set over a low heat. When apples have softened slightly, add ½ cup of brown sugar and 1 teaspoon of cinnamon. As soon as the sugar mixes with the butter forming a thick syrup, add back the sausage and cook for another ten minutes.

TARLETON OAKS' BREAKFAST CASSEROLE

1 skillet Belle's Best Buttery Biscuits (baked)
(See recipe under Bread Section)
1 9"x12" rectangular glass casserole
1 pound mild sausage (I use Tennessee Pride.)
1 medium Vidalia or sweet onion (chopped)
8-10 cherry tomatoes
½ cup green bell pepper
6 frozen hash brown patties (toasted and crumbled)
6 large eggs
1 cup half and half cream
1 tablespoon salt
1 teaspoon pepper
2 cups sharp cheddar cheese (shredded)
parsley flakes

Preheat oven to 350 degrees F. Grease 9"x12" casserole dish. The following will be put in layers. Crumble 6 biscuits and spread a thin layer on the bottom of the casserole. Cook and drain 1 pound mild sausage. Cool, crumble and layer on top of biscuits. Sauté onion and bell peppers and layer. Toast frozen hash brown patties in toaster, crumble and layer. Cut up 8-10 cherry tomatoes and layer. Combine 6 large eggs and 1 cup half and half cream. Add salt and pepper. Hand beat. Pour egg mixture over tomatoes. Top with 2 cups of shredded sharp cheddar cheese. Cover with aluminum foil and bake covered for 45 minutes. Uncover and cook for additional 15 minutes to brown. Remove from oven and sprinkle with parsley flakes. Let it cool for 5 minutes before cutting into 12 equal slices.

This recipe is perfect to prepare the night before, refrigerate and then pop in the oven the next morning. Yields 12 servings. Serve with fresh fruit such as strawberries, peaches and blueberries.

TARLETON OAKS' BREAKFAST PIZZA

1 package Boboli pre-baked pizza crust
1 pound pork sausage (I use Tennessee Pride.)
4 frozen hash browns (toaster type)
½ stick butter
5 eggs
¼ cup milk
1 cup sweet onions (chopped)
½ cup green bell pepper (chopped)
1 cup grape tomatoes (sliced)
sharp cheddar cheese (16 ounce package shredded)
salt and pepper to taste

Preheat oven to 375 degrees F. Place 1 Boboli on a round pizza pan. (Boboli is a pre-baked delicious pizza crust.) Sauté onion and bell peppers in ¼ stick butter over medium heat until soft (stirring constantly). Set aside in bowl. Brown and cook 1 pound pork sausage, drain and set aside. Put 4 frozen toaster-type hash browns in toaster at highest setting twice. Set aside. Scramble 5 eggs and ¼ cup milk in ¼ stick butter over medium heat (stirring constantly until soft and fluffy). Slice up 1 cup grape tomatoes and set aside.

Scatter drained pork sausage on top of Boboli Pizza Crust. Layer the following ingredients on top of sausage: crumbled hash browns, scrambled eggs, onion and bell pepper mixture, grape tomatoes. Salt and pepper to taste. Top all with 1 package of shredded sharp cheddar cheese. Cook approximately 10 minutes or until cheese is melted. Cut with pizza cutter and serve with fresh fruit.

Laura Hope Crews, who had also been a voice coach and theatrical director, began her acting career at the tender age of four. Laura appeared in 39 films, some Broadway productions and many plays. She took her acting profession very seriously and even asked for Bette Davis' dismissal in one production because of her "frivolous" attitude.

AUNT PITTYPAT'S APPLESAUCE COOKIES

1 ¼ cups sugar
1 1/3 cups shortening
3 eggs
2 teaspoons vanilla
1 cup applesauce
6 cups sifted flour
1 teaspoon baking soda
2 teaspoons baking powder
2 teaspoons nutmeg
1 teaspoon salt

Preheat oven to 375 degrees F. Cream together shortening, sugar, eggs and vanilla. Add applesauce and mix well. Add sifted dry ingredients and blend well. Drop by heaping tablespoons on greased cookie sheet and flatten. Then sprinkle with sugar and bake 10-12 minutes.

BELLE'S BUTTERMILK PIE

1 ¼ cups sugar
1 tablespoon all-purpose flour
5 eggs
1 cup buttermilk
1 tablespoon lemon juice
1 teaspoon vanilla
½ stick butter (melted)

Preheat oven to 350 degrees F. In a large bowl, combine sugar and flour. Beat in eggs and buttermilk until well blended. Stir in melted butter, lemon juice and vanilla. Pour filling into a 9" deep dish pie shell. Cook for one hour or until filling is set and the top is browned. Optional garnish: lemon slices and mint leaves. Let cool before cutting.

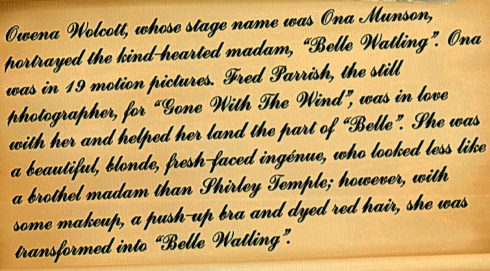

Owena Wolcott, whose stage name was Ona Munson, portrayed the kind-hearted madam, "Belle Watling". Ona was in 19 motion pictures. Fred Parrish, the still photographer, for "Gone With The Wind", was in love with her and helped her land the part of "Belle". She was a beautiful, blonde, fresh-faced ingénue, who looked less like a brothel madam than Shirley Temple; however, with some makeup, a push-up bra and dyed red hair, she was transformed into "Belle Watling".

When little Cammie King went into the studio to collect her check, she saw one of the "little people" wearing her costume. He was a stunt double and was used during the scene when Bonnie fell off the pony. Cammie ran up to her mother and screamed with excitement, "Mommy! Mommy! There's somebody wearing my costume and he's smoking a cigar!"

BONNIE'S BEST EVER CHOCOLATE CAKE

1 ½ cups sifted flour
3 tablespoons cocoa
1 teaspoon baking soda
1 cup sugar
½ teaspoon salt
5 tablespoons vegetable oil
1 tablespoon vinegar
1 teaspoon vanilla
1 cup cold water

Preheat oven to 350 degrees F. Sift together the following: flour, cocoa, baking soda, sugar and salt. Sift all of this into a greased square cake pan about 9"x9"x1". Make three holes in this dry mixture. Into one, pour the vegetable oil; into the next, pour vinegar; into the third, pour in vanilla. Next, pour 1 cup of cold water (filtered) over it all. Beat with a spoon until it's almost smooth and the flour is no longer visible. Bake for 30 minutes.

Love to Terry & Ted
Cammie King

Rand Brooks, who portrayed Charles Hamilton, the first husband of "Scarlett O'Hara", had a successful career in Hollywood. He worked in many westerns and was "Lucky Jenkins", the sidekick to "Hopalong Cassidy". He was "Ranger Andrews" in "Rocky Jones, Space Ranger" and "Corporal Boone" in the television series, "The Adventures of Rin Tin Tin". Rand was the first leading man to ever kiss Marilyn Monroe on the silver screen in "Ladies Of The Chorus". He was once married to Lois Laurel, the daughter of Stan Laurel (Laurel and Hardy). He later retired from acting, and, in 1966, started the company, Professional Ambulance Service, in Glendale, California, which won several awards beginning in 1977. Rand was worth millions when he sold it in 1995. He and his wife, Hermine, raised world-champion Andalusian horses in Santa Ynez, California when he retired.

CHARLES' FAVORITE COCONUT PIE

4 eggs
2 cups sugar
½ cup buttermilk
1 ½ cups butter (melted)
7 ounces coconut
2 pie shells

Preheat oven to 350 degrees F. In a large bowl, mix sugar and buttermilk. Add eggs and blend well. Scatter coconut over mix. Pour melted butter over coconut and mix together. Pour into pie shells and bake for 30-45 minutes or until set and golden brown.

GERALD'S GINGER BREAD

1 tablespoon butter
2 ½ cups flour
1 ½ teaspoons baking soda
½ cups butter
1 ¼ cups molasses
1 egg
1 ½ teaspoons cinnamon
1 ½ teaspoons allspice
1 cup very hot water

Preheat oven to 350 degrees F. Grease a 9" square baking pan with butter. In a large mixing bowl, combine flour, soda and spices. Cut in softened butter to the flour mixture with a fork. Combine molasses, egg and water in a small mixing bowl. Add the liquid ingredients to the dry ingredients and stir well. Pour the batter into a baking pan and bake 35-40 minutes or until a toothpick inserted into the center comes out clean.

Thomas Mitchell portrayed "Gerald O'Hara", Tara's Irish plantation owner. Thomas had been a newspaper reporter and a playwright before becoming an actor. He won an Academy Award for Best Supporting Actor in 1940 for "Stagecoach", an Emmy Award in 1952 for "Mayor Of The Town" as Best Dramatic Actor and a Tony Award in 1953 for Best Actor in a Musical. He was a hippophobe, someone afraid of horses. He had a clause written into his contract which relieved him from riding horses during filming.

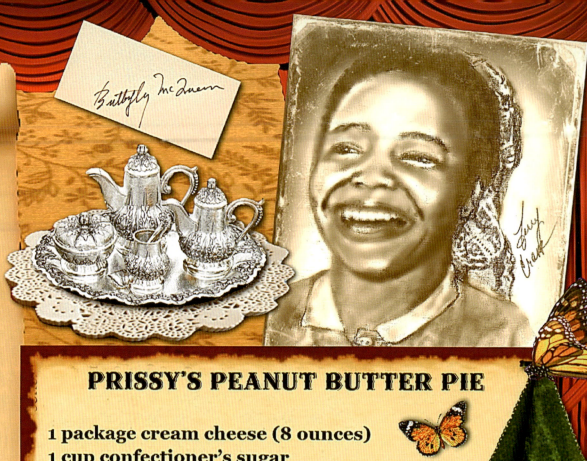

Thelma "Butterfly" McQueen portrayed the beloved character, "Prissy", in "Gone With The Wind". Thelma's nickname, "Butterfly", came from dancing the "Butterfly Ballet" in "A Midsummer Night's Dream" in 1935. When "Butterfly" learned that David Selznick was planning to film "Gone With The Wind", she set her heart on the role of "Prissy". One of Selznick's talent scouts, Mr. Bundamann, promptly turned her down with, "You're too old, too fat and too dignified for the part." Much later, after her failed audition, "Butterfly" had made a name for herself, and, much to her delight, was then sought out by the Selznick Studios and offered the role of "Prissy".

PRISSY'S PEANUT BUTTER PIE

1 package cream cheese (8 ounces)
1 cup confectioner's sugar
1 carton frozen non-dairy topping (9 ounces thawed)
1 9" graham cracker crumb or baked pie shell
¼ cup peanuts (finely chopped)
½ cup peanut butter
½ cup milk

Whip cream cheese until soft and fluffy. Beat in peanut butter and sugar. Slowly add milk, beating until well blended. Fold topping into mixture. Spoon into pie crust, sprinkle with peanuts. Freeze until firm. Yields 8-10 servings.

SCARLETT'S SKILLET CHOCOLATE PIE

Pie:

2 cups granulated sugar
4 rounded tablespoons flour
5 rounded tablespoons dry cocoa
½ cup butter
5 eggs (separated)
2 1/4 cups milk
2 pinches of sea salt
1 teaspoon vanilla
1 9-inch deep dish pie shell

Use uncooked pie shell and prepare shell by pricking the dough with a fork. Then bake in a 400 degree F oven for 10 minutes. Mix sugar, flour, salt and dry cocoa in bowl. Melt butter in a 10-inch iron skillet. Add dry mixture to melted butter and mix lightly. Combine egg yolks with milk and add to skillet mixture, stirring continually. Cook on low heat until mixture becomes thick. Remove from heat. Add vanilla and blend well. Then pour into a baked pie shell and cool.

Meringue:

5 egg whites (room temp)
Pinch of sea salt
Pinch of cream of tartar
1/4 teaspoon cider vinegar
1/2 teaspoon vanilla
10 tablespoons sugar

Let egg whites come to room temperature. Add a pinch of salt, a pinch of cream of tartar and ¼ teaspoon vinegar. Beat until stiff and add 10 tablespoons of sugar and vanilla until blended well. Pour carefully and evenly on top of cooled pie and swirl peaks. Bake at 350 degrees F for 15 minutes until meringue is brown.

When Fred first met Vivien Leigh, she and Selznick were negotiating her salary for the role of "Scarlett". She was offered a salary of $25,000. After portraying "Scarlett", Vivien was quoted, "'Scarlett' fascinated me, as she has fascinated so many others. She needed a good, healthy, old-fashioned spanking on a number of occasions, and I should have been delighted to give it to her. She was conceited, spoiled, arrogant—all those things, of course, are true of the character, but, she had courage and determination; that, I think, is why women must secretly admire her—even though we can't feel too happy about her many shortcomings."

The opening scene was filmed three times. The first time (lower left), the "Tarleton Twins'" hair was curly and bright red which made them look like a couple of Harpo Marxes! Also, "Scarlett" was wearing the green sprig barbecue dress. The second time (middle), the "Tarleton Twins'" hair was smoothed out and darkened. Notice, "Scarlett" was still wearing the green sprig dress. The entire movie had been shot when Susan Myrick, Selznick's Technical Advisor, told him, "David, you're going to have a hard time convincing the Daughters of the Confederacy that a girl that young would show that much bosom before 3 O'Clock!" So, Selznick, who was a perfectionist, called Vivien Leigh back from England and changed her costume to the white, virginal dress you now see in the opening scene. (bottom right) George Reeves ("Stuart") had begun filming a war picture and had shaved his head for the role; so Selznick had a wig made for George to wear. Fred Crane ("Brent") was visiting family and friends in New Orleans when he received a wire from Selznick asking him to return to re-shoot the opening scene. Much to Fred's dismay, they had to dye his hair for eight hours---all the while pulling, tugging and dying his hair multiple times with the hair dresser in tears trying to match George's wig!

About a week after Fred and I opened Tarleton Oaks Bed and Breakfast, we received a telephone call from our friend, the late Herb Bridges, a "Gone With The Wind" collector and author. He told us that he had some friends visiting him from out of town. They had expressed interest in meeting us and touring our home. I told him that we would be delighted to have them come by for a visit, and we set a time. Well, having learned that some of the guests were coming in from England, Fred and I decided to surprise them with a High Tea in the Tara Dining Room after the home tour. We went shopping for teas. Wow! We were overwhelmed with all the different flavors available! We didn't know what flavors they preferred, so, we bought every type of tea available at the local store and ingredients for finger sandwiches, assorted sweets and appetizers. It was our desire to give them a "Gone With The Wind" experience they would not soon forget. I also contacted our "Mammy" lookalike, Mildred Murphy, to see if she'd like to participate in the festivities.

When the day arrived, Herb and his friends walked to the front door and rang the doorbell. Mildred, dressed in full "Mammy" costume, answered the door and announced, "Welcome to Tarleton Oaks!" She slightly lifted the hem of her black dress and exposed her red, taffeta petticoat, making sure to rustle it as she turned. She called out, "Mistah Brent, Miz Terry, your guests iz here!" The woman from England was so overwhelmed that tears streamed freely down her face. With a refined, British accent, she said with excitement, "I cawn't believe I'm actually meeting Brent Tarleton!" We appeared at the door. As Fred held out his hand to greet her, she trembled all over. He tried to calm her nerves as she was visibly quite overcome with emotion. I invited them to join me in the Sitting Parlor so I could begin the tour of Tarleton Oaks. I told stories of the historic dwelling. (Our plan was to take them on the tour of the home, and, then, end in the Tara Dining Room where we would surprise them with the High Tea.)

Once we arrived at our final destination, we entered the large, formal dining room where the banquet table was elegantly set with china and silverware. Their eyes widened and mouths dropped as we invited them to sit down for some refreshments and partake in a High Tea. I asked the dear, British lady to sit next to Fred (which no doubt thrilled her since she was such a huge devotee of "Gone With The Wind"!) She continued to tremble and exclaimed, "Oh! I just cawn't believe I'm sitting next to Brent Tarleton!" Fred turned crimson with embarrassment. He smiled at her and continued to try to calm her nerves. We told them how honored we were to have them come out for a visit. As dear Mildred Murphy attended to our guests and served tasty, finger sandwiches, appetizers and sweets, I asked the guests, "What flavor of tea would you like? We have a delicious assortment from which to choose." The British woman replied in a somber voice, "Pardon me---but, we don't drink tea. We drink coffee." Fred and I looked at each other (as if we could read each other's mind thinking that we were going to be drinking a whole lot of tea for quite a few years.)

Tara Dining Room

We quickly brewed our delicious, Tarleton Oaks Breakfast Blend Coffee and enjoyed a lovely togetherness as we chatted for an hour or so through the remainder of their visit. We only hoped that it was as memorable for them as it was for us---an experience long remembered whenever we served hot tea to our guests at Tarleton Oaks.

Ann Rutherford portrayed "Carreen O'Hara" in "Gone With The Wind". Born to entertainer parents, she was a natural for the movies. She had been in numerous stage plays and films. Ann was especially popular as "Polly Benedict", Mickey Rooney's sweetheart in the "Andy Hardy" movie series. She also performed in the movie, "Orchestra Wives" with my former late father-in-law, Ray Eberle, the lead singer for the Glenn Miller Orchestra. Ray is my son, Tray's, grandfather.

CARREEN'S CHICKEN CURRY TEA SANDWICHES

2 cooked whole chicken breasts (finely chopped)
¼ cup nuts (finely chopped)
4 celery stalks (finely chopped)
salt to taste
mayonnaise (just enough to moisten)
curry powder to taste
16 slices best-quality white bread
½ cup unsalted butter (room temperature)

In a large bowl, combine chicken, nuts, celery, salt and mayonnaise; stir until well blended. Add curry powder. Spread one side of each piece of bread lightly with butter. Top the buttered side of 8 slices of bread with some of the chicken mixture and top with the remaining bread slices (buttered side down). Carefully cut the crusts from each sandwich. Cut the sandwiches in half diagonally and then cut in half again. Yields 8 whole sandwiches, 16 halves or 32 fourths.

CARREEN

ELLEN'S ARTICHOKE TEA SANDWICHES

2 (14 ounce) cans artichoke hearts in water (drained and chopped)
1¼ cups mayonnaise
1 tablespoon onion powder
1 teaspoon garlic powder
1 teaspoon dried parsley
½ teaspoon cayenne pepper
coarse salt and freshly-ground black pepper to taste
20 very thin slices premium white or wheat bread

In a medium bowl, combine chopped artichoke hearts, mayonnaise, onion powder, garlic powder, dried parsley and cayenne pepper. Season to taste with salt and pepper. Spread the mixture evenly over 10 slices of bread. Top each with the remaining 10 bread slices. Carefully cut the crusts from each sandwich. Cut the sandwiches in half diagonally. Then cut in half again. If desired, decorative shapes can be made with cookie cutters. Transfer the prepared sandwiches to a platter and wrap in plastic wrap. Refrigerate at least four hours or overnight to soften before serving. When ready to serve, remove from refrigerator. Uncover sandwiches just before serving. Yields 10 whole sandwiches, 20 halves or 40 fourths.

5"8" Barbara O'Neil, who portrayed "Ellen O'Hara", the mother of "Scarlett", "Suellen" and "Carreen", was only a few years older than Vivien Leigh when she portrayed the role of her mother in "Gone With The Wind". She appeared in 17 films from 1937 through 1957 and was a member of the University Players of Falmouth, Massachusetts. She was also an Artist-In-Residence at the University of Denver.

EMMY'S EGG & OLIVE TEA SANDWICHES

8 hard boiled eggs
small bottle of stuffed green olives
½ cup mayonnaise
salt and pepper to taste
1 tablespoon fresh dill weed (finely chopped)
6 tablespoons unsalted butter (room temperature)
20 slices of high quality white bread

Peel eggs and place into a medium bowl. Slice eggs and then coarsely mash them with the back of a fork. Finely chop the stuffed green olives and mix with eggs. Add mayonnaise, salt, pepper and dill; stir until well blended. Spread butter onto one side of each slice of bread. Spread the buttered side of 10 slices of bread with 2 tablespoons egg mixture. Top with remaining slices of bread (buttered side down). Carefully cut the crusts from sandwich. Cut in half diagonally, then, cut in half again. If desired, decorative shapes can be made with cookie cutters. Yields 10 whole sandwiches, 20 halves or 40 fourths.

Pretty Isabel Jewell, who portrayed "Emmy Slattery" in "Gone With The Wind", was in numerous films from 1932 until 1957 and performed on stage in two productions, "Blessed Event" in 1932 and "Johnny 2x4" in 1942. She had been arrested for writing bad checks in Las Vegas, Nevada in 1959 and for drunk driving in 1961. Tragically, Isabel passed away in Hollywood, California in 1972 while she was living in poverty as a street person.

Isabel Jewell

SUELLEN'S SMOKED SALMON SANDWICHES

¼ cup mayonnaise
1 tablespoon green onion (minced)
1 tablespoon fresh dill weed (minced)
1 tablespoon capers (drained)
1 teaspoon prepared horseradish
pepper to taste
2 teaspoons butter (room temperature)
8 slices pumpernickel bread
4 to 6 slices of smoked salmon
12 cucumber slices (thinly sliced)

In a small bowl, combine mayonnaise, green onion, dill weed, capers, horseradish and pepper; then set aside. Spread butter thinly over pumpernickel bread slices; spread mayonnaise mixture on each bread slice. Divide salmon and cucumber slices evenly over 4 slices of bread. Top with remaining bread slices. Cut each sandwich in half diagonally or in quarters. Yields 4 whole sandwiches, 8 halves or 16 fourths.

Evelyn Keyes portrayed "Suellen O'Hara" in "Gone With The Wind". In one of my first conversations with her on the telephone, she said, "You know, Terry Lynn, I've been the leading lady in almost 50 films, but the only role I am ever remembered for is "Suellen" in "Gone With The Wind! Why do you think there's so much fascination with that movie?!"

MEATS & MAIN ENTREES

Leslie Howard

ASHLEY'S BARBECUED CHICKEN

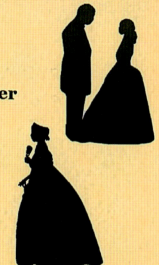

3 tablespoons catsup
¼ cup vinegar
½ cup water
¼ teaspoon black pepper
2 tablespoons sugar
½ cup chopped onion
1 tablespoon mustard
½ cup cooking oil
salt to taste
1 2-2 ½ pound chicken
flour

Combine catsup, vinegar, water, pepper, sugar, onion, mustard, ¼ cup cooking oil and ½ teaspoon salt in pan; simmer until onion is cooked. Dredge chicken in mixture of flour and salt; brush with remaining oil. Place chicken in baking dish. Pour sauce over chicken. Bake for 3 hours at 350 degrees F, turning often. Yields 4 servings.

While Leslie Howard was an excellent actor, he did not want to play the role of the honor-bound, disillusioned, intellectual, southern gentleman, "Ashley Wilkes". Leslie felt he was too old for the role. However, Selznick knew he would be perfect for the part and "dangled a carrot in front of him" saying "Leslie, if you play "Ashley Wilkes" in "Gone With The Wind", then I'll let you co-produce, direct and star in "Intermezzo". This was a role Selznick knew Leslie wanted. He agreed and starred in both movies simultaneously.

Beautiful Olivia de Havilland portrayed the meek and sweet "Melanie Wilkes" in "Gone With The Wind". While Olivia did not win an Academy Award for Best Supporting Actress for "Gone With The Wind", she did, however, win two Academy Awards for Best Actress and two New Film Critics' Awards for Best Feminine Performance. She was quoted as saying, "Playing good girls in the 30's was difficult when the fad was to play bad girls. Actually, I think playing bad girls is a bore. I have always had more luck with good girl roles, because they require more from an actress."

MELANIE'S MARINATED STEAK

2 cloves of garlic (crushed)
½ cup soy sauce
¼ cup brown sugar
2 tablespoons olive oil
¼ teaspoon pepper
4 T-Bone Steaks

Combine all ingredients (except steaks) in a jar and shake well. Pour over steaks. Marinate steaks for at least 1 hour or preferably overnight. Broil steaks over charcoal or in oven, basting often with marinade. Cook steaks to desired doneness. Makes 4 servings.

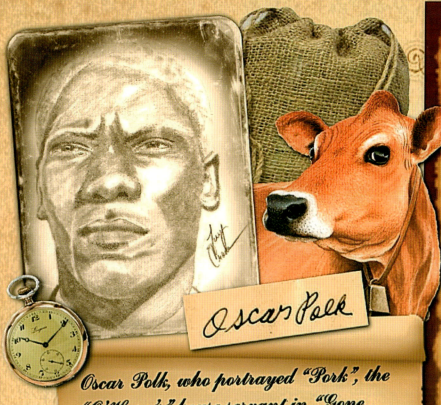

Oscar Polk

Oscar Polk, who portrayed "Pork", the "O'Hara's" house servant in "Gone With The Wind", appeared in six motion pictures between the years 1936 and 1943. He also appeared in numerous plays. While he was very well cast in the role of "Pork", he was criticized by some of his black brethren for playing the "demeaning role of a slave" and called him "an Uncle Tom". His answer was, "You have to know where we were to know where we are. That's history!"

PORK'S PLANTATION PORK CHOPS

6 center cut pork chops (1/2" thick)
1 teaspoon sugar
3 tablespoons soy sauce
1 tablespoon sherry
2 teaspoons flour
3 tablespoons peanut oil
2 cups onions (vertically sliced)
2 tablespoons cold water

Trim off the excess fat from pork chops. Pound each chop to 1/8" thickness. Place on greased baking sheet. Combine sugar, 2 tablespoons soy sauce and sherry. Spoon over chops (coating both sides well). Sift flour onto both sides of chops. Set aside. Preheat large skillet for 30 seconds on high heat. Add one tablespoon peanut oil. Add sliced onion. Reduce heat to moderate. Stir fry until onions are tender for approximately 5 minutes. Remove onions. Set aside. Pour remaining 2 tablespoons peanut oil into skillet. Fry chops over moderate heat until slightly browned, about one minute on each side. Spoon onions over chops. Add remaining 1 tablespoon soy sauce and water. Cover, reduce heat to low and cook about twenty minutes or until chops are tender. Transfer to heated serving platter covering chops with onions. Serve with rice. Yields 4 servings.

David Selznick's first choice for the part of "Rhett Butler" was Gary Cooper, but he turned it down. Selznick then knew he had to have Clark Gable who was under contract with MGM Studios. In his negotiations with MGM, Selznick agreed to give them Distribution Rights and 50% of the profits in exchange for a loan of $1,250,000 and Gable. When Louis B. Mayer told Gable that they were loaning him to portray "Rhett Butler", he was quite upset. He didn't feel he could do the part justice and was highly intimidated by the character because the book was such a world-wide success. After much cajoling, Gable cautiously accepted the role. Louis B. Mayer gave Gable's wife, Ria Langham, $286,000 so that she would agree to grant him a divorce. (He wanted to marry Carole Lombard.) He also asked for his choice of directors, a salary of $120,000 and working hours from 9am-5pm. "Rhett Butler" would become Clark Gable's favorite role.

RHETT'S NEW ORLEANS POT ROAST

1 4-pound pot roast
½ teaspoon pepper
½ teaspoon cloves
½ teaspoon mace
½ teaspoon allspice
1 teaspoon chili powder
1 tablespoon sale
1 clove garlic (minced)
2 tablespoons lemon juice
1 tablespoon vinegar
1 ½ cup cooking oil
1 can tomato sauce
2 cups water
2-3 bay leaves

Rub meat with combined seasonings and garlic. Combine lemon juice, vinegar and ½ cup oil; pour over meat (covering well). Refrigerate several hours or overnight, turning occasionally. Coat with flour, sear in remaining oil until brown. Reduce heat, add marinade, tomato sauce, water and bay leaves. Simmer slowly until done. Yields 6 servings.

TWELVE OAKS' SHORT RIB BARBECUE

3-4 pounds beef short ribs
3 tablespoons fat
1 package onion soup mix
¼ cup vinegar
2 tablespoons brown sugar
1 cup catsup
½ cup water
1 teaspoon prepared mustard
1 teaspoon salt

Parboil ribs until tender; then brown in hot fat in a Dutch oven. Combine remaining ingredients; pour over ribs. Cover and simmer for 2 hours, turning occasionally. Yields 6 servings.

This photograph is from the scene of the barbecue at "Twelve Oaks", the plantation home of "Ashley Wilkes". This scene was actually filmed at Busch Gardens in Pasadena, California and not on the movie lot at Selznick International Pictures in Culver City, California. All scenes, but this one, were filmed at Selznick Studios; however, there is a small clip of a windmill at the beginning of the movie that was filmed in Arkansas.

Top Photo: Rand Brooks as "Charles Hamilton" and Vivien Leigh as "Scarlett O'Hara"
Bottom Left: Sketch of Leslie Howard as "Ashley Wilkes" by Terry Lynn Crane
Bottom Right: Sketch of Olivia deHavilland as "Melanie Wilkes" by Terry Lynn Crane

DOLLY'S EIGHT LAYER SALAD

1 small head of Iceberg Lettuce (shredded)
1 cup chopped celery
1 sweet onion (finely chopped)
1 large bag of frozen English Peas (uncooked)
2 cups mayonnaise
½ cup sour cream
2 tablespoons sugar
4 ounces shredded Cheddar Cheese
1 pound bacon

Fry bacon crisp. Drain bacon on a paper towel. Crumble bacon and set aside. Put the following ingredients in by layers in to a crystal or clear bowl (for presentation).

Layer 1: shredded lettuce
Layer 2: chopped celery
Layer 3: chopped onion
Layer 4: uncooked English peas
Layer 5: mayonnaise mixed with sour cream
Layer 6: sprinkle sugar over mayonnaise
Layer 7: shredded Cheddar Cheese
Layer 8: sprinkle crumbled bacon over top

Refrigerate for 24 hours. Yields 8-10 servings.

Patti Woodward, whose stage name was Jane Darwell, portrayed "Mrs. Dolly Merriwether" in "Gone With The Wind". She had originally intended on being a circus performer, but her parents strongly objected. She compromised and changed her name to Jane Darwell (so that she wouldn't embarrass her family). She appeared in more than 170 films and won an Academy Award in 1941 for Best Supporting Actress for her portrayal of "Ma Joad" opposite Henry Fonda in the movie, "The Grapes of Wrath". After Jane had retired from acting, Walt Disney personally visited her at the Motion Picture Country Home and asked her to come out of retirement for the role of the beloved "Bird Lady" in the movie, "Mary Poppins". She accepted the role and "Mary Poppins" became her final motion picture.

Jane Darwell

Alicia Rhett

Alicia Rhett was a contender for the role of "Scarlett". She was originally discovered while performing in a play in Charleston, South Carolina by Kay Brown, the woman who insisted that David Selznick purchase the screen rights to <u>Gone With The Wind</u>. Alicia, instead, was offered the role of "India Wilkes", the sister of "Ashley" and bore a striking resemblance to Leslie Howard. Alicia, an accomplished artist, passed the time between scenes sketching many of the "Gone With The Wind" actors and actresses in their costumes.

INDIA'S CREAM OF BROCCOLI SOUP

2 tablespoons butter
1 onion (chopped)
1 stalk celery chopped)
3 cups chicken broth
8 cups broccoli florets

3 tablespoons butter
3 tablespoons flour
2 cups milk
salt and ground-black pepper to taste

Melt 2 tablespoons butter in medium-sized stock pot. Sauté onion and celery until tender. Add broccoli and broth, cover and simmer for 10 minutes. Pour the soup into a blender, filling the pitcher no more than halfway full. Hold down the lid and carefully start the blender, using a few quick pulses to get the soup moving before leaving it on to puree. Puree in batches until smooth and pour into a clean pot. Alternately, you can use a hand blender and puree the soup right in the cooking pot.

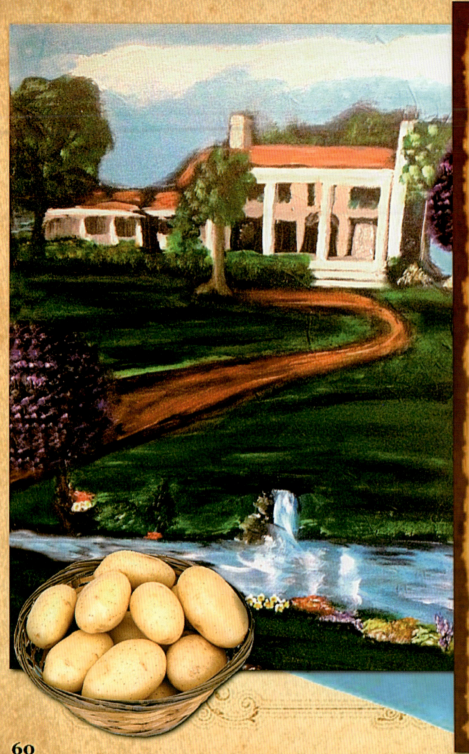

PLANTATION POTATO SALAD

6-8 large potatoes
4-5 heaping tablespoons mayonnaise
2 tablespoons prepared mustard
1 medium onion (diced)
1 red bell pepper (diced)
1 stalk celery (sliced into thin wedges)
4 large kosher pickles (diced)
salt and pepper to taste
parsley
lettuce leaves (optional)

Peel potatoes, cut into bite-sized pieces and boil for about 15 minutes or until tender. Rinse boiled potatoes in cold water to cool. Place potatoes in a large bowl. Add mayonnaise and mustard. Blend gingerly to just coat potatoes. Fold bell pepper, celery, onion and pickles gently into potato mixture. Add salt and pepper to taste. Garnish with parsley. Place in refrigerator overnight to marry the flavors.

(For a beautiful presentation, you can serve individually on a salad plate. Place washed lettuce leaf on salad plate and top with Plantation Potato Salad. Garnish with parsley or paprika.)

BRENT'S BAKED BEANS

1 pound lean ground beef
3 cans pork and beans
1 sweet onion (chopped)
1 green bell pepper (chopped)
1 tablespoon Worcestershire Sauce
1 small bottle hickory barbecue sauce
¾ cup light brown sugar
1 tablespoon prepared mustard
4 dashes of Louisiana Hot Sauce

Preheat oven to 350 degrees F. Brown ground beef and drain grease; set aside. In ceramic bean pot, combine pork and beans, onion, bell pepper, Worcestershire Sauce, hickory barbecue sauce, light brown sugar, mustard and Louisiana Hot Sauce. Carefully fold in drained ground beef and mix thoroughly. Bake in oven for 1 hour. This takes ordinary baked beans to a new level. Mmmmmmmmm good!

Fred Crane wasn't looking for a job, had not read Margaret Mitchell's novel and had never been to a movie studio when he was cast as "Brent Tarleton" in "Gone With The Wind". Originally, he was cast as both "Tarleton Twins", but it would have required them to do a process shot and restrict the movement in the scenes. A couple of weeks after Fred had been cast, they found George Reeves who looked enough like Fred that they became the "Tarleton Boys" in the movie. This is one of my favorite photos of Fred. He was in this same attitude during the smoking room scene at "Twelve Oaks" where he confronts "Rhett Butler" and has dialog with actor, Clark Gable.

CARREEN'S GLAZED CARROTS

2 cups sliced carrots
1 cup orange juice
½ cup granulated sugar
1 tablespoon cornstarch
Dash of nutmeg

Cook carrots until tender and drain. Mix remaining ingredients in separate pan and cook until the sauce thickens. Pour the sauce over carrots and let stand for a short time. Serve hot. Yields 6 servings.

Adorable Ann Rutherford was aware of David Selznick's budget constraints and schedule for "Gone With The Wind". In her considerate way, she told Selznick, "You don't have to go to that expense for my shoes, David. No one would see them anyway." Selznick replied, "But let me ask you how you would feel if you didn't have your costume complete?"

DR. MEADE'S DANDY DUTCH LETTUCE

1 head Iceberg Lettuce
2 hard-boiled eggs (chopped)
2 small sweet onions (chopped)
½ cup diced bacon (cooked)
½ cup vinegar
1 tablespoon sugar
1 teaspoon salt
bacon drippings
4 potatoes, boiled

Let lettuce leaves stand in cold water for approximately one hour and then drain well on paper towels. In baking dish, alternate layers of lettuce, bacon, eggs, onions and mashed potatoes. Add vinegar, sugar and salt to bacon fat and heat to boiling. Pour over layers and serve hot. Yields 8 servings.

Harry Davenport was born in 1866 in New York, New York, the year after The War Between The States had ended. He was the oldest actor in "Gone With The Wind" and portrayed Dr. J. A. Meade, a renowned physician and leader in Atlanta. Harry made his stage debut at the age of 5 and came from a long line of actors and actresses spanning a 100+ year period. After a successful stage career, he debuted in silent films in 1914. A roster of his stage plays and films from 1871-1934 took up two full pages in 1934. Along with Eddie Foy, in 1913, he co-founded the Actors Equity Association, an American labor union for actors.

Top Photo: Fred Crane ("Brent Tarleton") is on the left, Susan Myrick (Technical Advisor) is in the middle and George Bessolo, who changed his name to George Reeves, ("Stuart Tarleton") is on the right.

In the book, *White Columns Over Hollywood*, Susan Myrick wrote, "George Bessolo is one twin and Fred Crane is the other, but nobody knows which is who. They both have mops of red hair, and, though they are not exactly alike, they are both so funny that we didn't bother to remember one from t'other."

Bottom Photo: Fred Crane ("Brent Tarleton") is on the left and George Reeves ("Stuart Tarleton") is on the right.